YOURS FOR THE GIVING: SPIRITUAL GIFTS

Revised Edition

BARBARA JOINER

New Hope Publishers

Birmingham, Alabama

New Hope Publishers
P. O. Box 12065
Birmingham, AL 35202-2065

Dewey Decimal Classification: 248.4
Subject Headings: GIFTS (THEOLOGY)
                  CHRISTIAN LIFE

Cover design by Debra Eubanks Riffe
Back cover photo by Pupil of the Eye Photography/John Schoenfeld

ISBN: 1-56309-248-4
N993106 • 0399 • 10M1

TABLE OF CONTENTS

INTRODUCTION

I wrote the first edition of *Yours for the Giving: Spiritual Gifts* in 1985. It was released the following year. Interest in spiritual gifts was not overwhelming—to say the least.

With a great deal of help, I ferreted out 48 books (from the beginning of time) and a clutch of articles. Some were very helpful, some less so. I read, laboriously, two encyclopedias (my description) on gifts. One had 52 gifts that were examined minutely. Each chapter concluded without any help for the reader to determine her gifts.

At that point, I decided that *Yours for the Giving* would have three primary goals:

- Describe each gift thoroughly, but briefly.
- Provide an inventory to assist the reader in finding her gifts.
- Encourage the reader to use her gifts.

Imagine my amazement when people actually purchased the book—in great numbers. Moreover, they flocked to hear it taught. Not only that, but a number of writers wrote excellent books about spiritual gifts in the following years. Interest in spiritual gifts blossomed.

So why has this fledgling book hung on? In the 1990s it was discontinued. A cry went up—I'm not sure how many cries, but enough that the book was republished and it continued to sell. And lo, here in 1999 a new and improved revision is presented to you!

It has a gorgeous new cover and—thanks be to God—a better picture of the author on the back cover! Inside some of the stories are different, but the gifts are the same ones God has always given. The excellent inventory designed by Dr. John Hendrix is still in place. And I still strongly encourage the reader to use her gifts to serve the Lord. Because gifts are for giving.

CHAPTER 1

ALL GOD'S CHILDREN GOT THE SPIRIT

They were behind closed doors, locked gates, terrified! They waited for the heavy thud of marching feet coming to take them to a cross. It was all over. Hope was gone. Jesus was dead.

At first it was whispered, "Alive!" Then they shouted through the streets of Jerusalem: "Jesus is alive!" What Jesus had said He would do, He had done. He had conquered death! He had come out of that rock-hewn tomb! They touched Him; they ate with Him in that seaside picnic. They listened and He said, "I'll never leave you."

Jesus had already told the disciples about the Holy Spirit. John 14 pulses with the promise. Jesus said, "And I will ask the Father, and He will give you another Counselor to be with you forever" (John 14:16).

How well Jesus knew the disciples. He knew the crucifixion would shatter them. He said, "I will not leave you as orphans; I will come to you" (John 14:18).

The crucifixion did shatter the disciples. Yet only weeks later, those "orphans" started turning the world upside down. Who changed 11 defeated men into earthshaking, fiery apostles? Who sent them out to challenge governments, powers, even death itself? Who changed an illiterate, stubborn, denying fisherman into the mighty preacher of Pentecost? The Strengthener, the Holy Spirit.

Who put hope in their hearts, as well as understanding? The Counselor, the Holy Spirit.

Who spoke to their hearts and speaks to hearts today and convicts of sin? The Intercessor, the Holy Spirit.

Who comforted the disciples and comforts us today? The Comforter, the Holy Spirit.

Who gave Peter the words to say, the understanding to interpret Old Testament Scriptures, the fervor that caused 3,000 to respond? The Helper, the Holy Spirit.

The disciples began to understand the power, the wonder of the Spirit, and the tremendous price tag attached to His coming. The Holy Spirit could not come until Jesus had been crucified, resurrected, and ascended into heaven.

During the 40 days after the crucifixion, Jesus continued to teach the disciples about the kingdom of God. He reminded them that the Holy Spirit would empower them to do their work which was to spread the gospel. Remember these words? "And when the Holy Spirit comes on you, you will be able to be my witnesses in Jerusalem, all over Judea and Samaria, even to the ends of the world" (Acts 1:8 *The Message*).

Luke writes that immediately after Jesus said this, He was lifted up to heaven (Acts 1:9).

As Jesus had said He would, the Holy Spirit came. Acts 2 records the outpouring of the Spirit: the rushing wind, the mass of flame, the miracle of communication to all the people at Pentecost in their own language. Peter preached with astounding power. And the Holy Spirit began His mighty work of convicting sinners of their sin. When the people heard Peter's preaching, they were deeply troubled and said to Peter and the other apostles, "Brothers! Brothers! So now what do we do?" (Acts 2:37 *The Message*).

Peter's answer was, "Change your life. Turn to God and be baptized, each of you, in the name of Jesus Christ, so that your sins are forgiven. Receive the gift of the Holy Spirit" (Acts 2:38 *The Message*).

This promise was true at Pentecost and it is true today, because Peter continued to say, "The promise is targeted to you and your children, but also to all who are far away" (Acts 2:39 *The Message*).

These verses make it clear that at the time of conversion, Jesus gives us the Holy Spirit. And when the Holy Spirit comes into our lives, He gives us gifts—our spiritual gifts. Stuart Calvert in her book *Uniquely Gifted* states, "The Holy Spirit is a Gift Giver. He assigned us one or more gifts the day we were born again."

The rest of the good news is that this is only the beginning.

CHAPTER 2

ALL GOD'S CHILDREN GOT GIFTS

When Jesus gave the disciples the job of telling the world about Him, it was no easy task. He said, "Go"; "Make disciples"; "Baptize"; "Teach." Jesus also knew that bands of believers would come together in His name to worship, fellowship, and serve. In order for God's people to survive, for His church to grow, for the world to know, God gave every one of the believers gifts.

When does this giving take place? The writer of Hebrews says that when we are saved we are given gifts—each one of us (Heb. 2:3–4). Our salvation is a free gift. It is undeserved. "For it is by grace you have been saved, through faith—and this not from yourselves, it is the gift of God" (Eph. 2:8). Our spiritual gifts are grace gifts too. We do not deserve them. We do not choose them. God decides and gives.

Paul wrote and taught a great deal about gifts. That should be expected because Paul was a church planter. To the church at Ephesus he said, "But to each one of us grace has been given as Christ apportioned it" (Eph. 4:7). To the Corinthian church he said, "Now to each one the manifestation of the Spirit is given for the common good" (1 Cor. 12:7).

Let me emphasize again: We do not choose our own gift or gifts. In fact, we should not even ask for them. First Corinthians 12:11 says, "All these are the work of one and the same Spirit, and He gives them to each one, just as He determines."

Ralph Neighbour, author of *This Gift of Mine*, explains, "God Himself gives His children gifts. He doesn't need or accept our advice. He knows us better than we know ourselves. So He chooses the perfect gifts for each of us."

Paul patiently and graphically explained how the gifts were given by comparing the members of the church body to the different parts of the human body. First Corinthians 12:14–21 is a simple anatomy lesson of the human body and God's church. The point made is that even though the foot, the eye, the ear, the hand, and the other parts are different, they all make up one body and each is essential. In the church we are all different with different gifts, but all are essential to God's church.

So what are these spiritual gifts? Let's search them out in God's Word. Even reading directly from the Bible we find no cut-and-dried listing. But let's look at each "gift" passage and mark the gifts. A bold-faced word will indicate that most consider it a gift. An italicized word is considered a gift by some. After the Scripture marking, a master list will follow.

8

ROMANS 12:6–13

6 We have different gifts according to the grace given us. If a man's gift is **prophesying**, let him use it in proportion to his faith.

7 If it is **serving**, let him serve; if it is **teaching**, let him teach;

8 if it is **encouraging**, let him encourage; if it is **contributing** to the needs of others, let him give generously; if it is **leadership**, let him govern diligently; if it is **showing mercy**, let him do it cheerfully.

9 *Love* must be sincere. Hate what is evil; cling to what is good.

10 Be devoted to one another in brotherly love. Honor one another above yourselves. Never be lacking in zeal, but keep your spiritual *fervor*, serving the Lord. Be joyful in *hope*, patient in affliction, faithful in *prayer*. Share with God's people who are in need. Practice *hospitality*.

FIRST CORINTHIANS 12:8–10,28–30

8 To one there is given through the spirit the **message of wisdom**, to another the **message of knowledge** by means of the same Spirit,

9 to another **faith** by the same Spirit, to another gifts of **healing** by that one Spirit,

10 to another **miraculous powers**, to another **prophecy**, to another the ability to **distinguish between spirits**, to another the ability to **speak in different kinds of tongues**, and to still another the **interpretation of tongues**.

28 And in the church God has appointed first of all **apostles**, second **prophets**, third **teachers**, then workers of miracles, also those having gifts of healing, those able to **help others**, those with the gifts of **administration**, and those speaking in different kinds of tongue.

29 Are all apostles? Are all prophets? Are all teachers? Do all work miracles?
30 Do all have gifts of healing? Do all speak in tongues? Do all interpret?

EPHESIANS 4:11
11 It was He who gave some to be **apostles**, some to be **prophets**, some to be **evangelists** and some to be **pastors** and **teachers**.

FIRST PETER 4:10–11
10 Each one should use whatever gift he has received to serve others, faithfully administering God's grace in its various forms.
11 If anyone **speaks**, he should do it as one speaking the very words of God. If anyone **serves**, he should do it with the strength God provides, so that in all things God may be praised through Jesus Christ. To Him be the glory and the power for ever and ever. Amen.

MASTER LIST
1. Prophecy (Preaching)
2. Ministering (Service, Helps)
3. Teaching
4. Exhorting
5. Giving (Sharing)
6. Ruling (Leading, Government, Administration)
7. Mercy
8. Love
9. Fervency (Enthusiasm)
10. Hope
11. Prayer
12. Hospitality

13. Wisdom
14. Knowledge
15. Faith
16. Healing
17. Miracles
18. Discerning of spirits
19. Tongues
20. Interpretation of tongues
21. Apostleship
22. Evangelism
23. Pastoring

Now that I have committed myself to a master list, let me start backpedaling. Is the list correct? It is not like any other list I've seen. There are several gifts listed that are found on only a few lists. Love is one such gift. Love is a part of the fruit of the Spirit (see Gal. 5:22). Can love be considered a gift as well? I've left it on the list for several reasons. For one thing, I know some who are gifted at loving. Plus faith is often listed as a gift. Yet faith also is a fruit of the Spirit. The instrument we will use in chapter 4 to search for gifts lists love. So love, of necessity, remains on my list!

Prayer is on my list. Every believer has prayed, and must pray. Is it proper to list prayer as a gift? Some authorities say no. Because I know people with this gift I leave this gift on my master list.

Some would list hospitality under the gift of ministry or helps. I have left hospitality on my list.

Some would add categories to my list. I have combined service and helps, although others would separate these two categories. I have combined leadership and administration, while others would see them as two distinct categories.

Rick Yohn lists craftsmanship and music in his book *Discover Your Spiritual Gift and Use It*. I would classify craftsmanship under service. Music is harder for me to place. When it is beyond talent, music can preach and share. Are any of the listings of spiritual gifts complete? Bible scholars do not agree.

Well-known Bible teacher Dr. G. Campbell Morgan said, "In the Scriptures of the New Covenant we find different lists of the 'gifts' bestowed upon His church by the risen and glorified Lord. It has often been pointed out that no two of these lists are exactly alike. There is deep suggestiveness and great beauty in this fact. We are all strangely prone to mechanism, and are too fond of tabulating systematically even the things of God. There would have been some sort of satisfaction in having an exhaustive list of His gifts. Yet how sad would it have been, for inevitably we should have spent much time in seeking to place each other by our gifts, or pitying such as seemed to possess none. The gifts were never tabulated exhaustively because they cannot be exhausted; and while today some of the earliest are not found, many new and precious ones are ours."[1]

But let's take what light we do have and attempt to define and describe the gifts before us. Then we can take this light and see how we can use our gifts in missions. For Paul did say, "I do not want you to be ignorant" (1 Cor. 12:1).

PROPHECY (PREACHING)

Until God's Word was completed it was necessary for prophets to give special revelations and reliable guidance. But since the Bible has revealed the coming of Christ, His crucifixion, and resurrection, prophecy now means proclamation of this Word.

Bible scholars say that prophesying is generally accepted

today as preaching the written Word of God with the aid of the Holy Spirit.

Prophecy requires faith to operate effectively. The deeper the faith, the greater the prophecy. People with tremendous faith move the hearts and minds of listeners and are revered by many.

Some, however, cling to the concept that prophecy is, as of old, a divine utterance from God that He speaks to certain gifted people.

Still others claim that prophecy is receiving and speaking direct revelations from God. But they believe that Scripture is now God's revelation and therefore no other revelations are given. Prophecy, they conclude, is no longer present today.

I believe prophecy is definitely present today. Prophetic preaching is alive and well.

MINISTERING (SERVICE, HELPS)

Ministry or serving is a common gift for everyday living. It means serving people with basic things that people need—like food, clothing, shelter, care, love, and a million other things.

We all do things for others, but those with the gift for service have something extra. They do it with the right spirit, the Holy Spirit.

Another characteristic about the gift of ministry is that the gifted person often serves behind the scenes, just doing the necessary.

You may recall that the Scripture tells of Dorcas, a servant who was raised from the dead. No preacher or evangelist was considered that indispensable!

Jesus served others and taught His disciples to serve others. We must be willing to do so as well or the church lacks integrity and denies its Lord.

TEACHING

Teaching is one of the essential tasks of the Great Commission: "Teaching them to observe all things whatsoever I have commanded you" (Matt. 28:20 KJV). The gift of teaching includes instructing, guiding, and nurturing Christians in God's Word.

A preacher explained that preaching is directed to the will, teaching is directed to the understanding. Gifted teachers capably explain what the Word of God actually says.

William McRae points out that a person with the gift of teaching is marked by two characteristics: (1) a keen interest in the personal study of the Word and in the disciplines involved in studying the Scriptures; (2) the capacity to communicate clearly the truths and applications of the Word so that others may learn and profit.

One conclusion: Without teaching, there is no discipleship (Matt. 28:19–20). Without teaching, you have no spiritual maturity (Col. 1:28).

EXHORTING

Exhortation means to speak out helpfully. It is the gift of counseling, the ability to give comforting and healing words to others. A person with this gift is an encourager.

John Hendrix states that "exhortation does not dwell on weaknesses and shortcomings." Instead it builds up, encourages, and strengthens another to do his best.

My favorite description of exhortation is Leslie Flynn's in his book *19 Gifts of the Spirit*: "The gift of exhortation involves the supernatural ability to come alongside to help, to strengthen the weak, re-assure the wavering, buttress the buffeted, steady the faltering, console the troubled, encourage the halting."

No wonder that exhortation is called the gift closest to the nature of the Holy Spirit Himself.

GIVING (SHARING)

Every Christian should be a giver. In fact God has told us that He expects a tithe. A person with the gift of giving, however, goes beyond the requirement.

You don't have to be wealthy to have the gift of giving. All that is required is simplicity. Paul says in Romans 12:8 that we are to give with simplicity. That means from an open heart, freely, with delight, with love.

Giving goes beyond our money. Luke 3:11 states, "The man with two tunics should share with him who has none, and the one who has food should do the same."

Giving should be based not on what one has, but on the faith that God will supply all our needs from His treasury. That's what St. Francis of Assisi was talking about when he said, "For it is in giving that we receive."

RULING (LEADING, GOVERNMENT, ADMINISTRATION)

Perhaps too much is included in my grouping above. A person may indeed have the gift of leading and be lacking in administration. One may be an excellent administrator and lack leadership ability. But the two attributes combined in His power are formidable.

If you want to get things done and get them done well, call on a person with the gift of administration.

Administration has been defined as the God-given capacity to organize and administer with such efficiency and spirituality that not only is the project brought to a satisfactory conclusion, but it is done harmoniously and with evident blessing, says McRae.

Many see leadership as a separate gift from that of administration. Rick Yohn states, "The gift of administration is probably a refinement of the general gift of leading." He explains that "experience demonstrates that not all leaders are good administrators. The leader who does the work by himself and refuses to delegate responsibility isn't a good administrator even though he may get the job done."

Other writers use words such as *motivator, model,* and *servant* to describe gifted leaders.

MERCY

Rich Yohn says that a person gifted with showing mercy sparkles like a diamond against a dark background of indifference. For mercy is the ability to work joyfully with those whom the majority ignores: the deformed, crippled, mentally challenged, sick, aged, or mentally ill.

Mercy is not just kindness from someone's heart, it is a divine love. A person gifted in mercy does not steel herself in the face of another's pain. Instead, she is drawn to her suffering brother. She feels compelled to help. She must do something about it.

LOVE

"And now these three remain: faith, hope and love. But the greatest of these is love" (1 Cor. 13:13). Paul emphasized to the Corinthian church the tremendous importance of love. All else without love is empty, meaningless. The greatest preaching and teaching is only noise without love. The most sacrificial service is busy work without love.

God is love. It is His nature, His character. As we strive to be more like Him, we become more loving.

Love is more than a gift. It is a part of the fruit of the

Spirit (Gal. 5:22). It is the way the world tests us to see if we belong to the Father.

Love is not optional for a Christian. For Christ said, "By this all men will know that you are my disciples, if you love one another" (John 13:35). Some are especially gifted in love, but all of us must try each day to become more loving.

FERVENCY (ENTHUSIASM)

The Message paraphrase of Romans 12:11 is to the point: "Don't burn out; keep yourselves fueled and aflame. Be alert servants of the Master, cheerfully expectant." Paul was paying tribute to the gift of enthusiasm or fervency in this verse. Other words for fervent are *eager* and *seething* and *boiling over!* I've always thought the exclamation mark was made for the enthusiastic!!!

Hendrix says the enthusiastic take seriously the words of Jesus. "Here's another way to put it: You're here to be light, bringing out the God-colors in the world. God is not a secret to be kept. We're going public with this, as public as a city on a hill. If I make you light-bearers, you don't think I'm going to hide you under a bucket, do you? I'm putting you on a light stand. Now that I've put you there on a hill-top, on a light stand—shine! Keep open house; be generous with your lives. By opening up to others, you'll prompt people to open up with God, this generous Father in heaven" (Matt. 5:14–16 *The Message*).

HOPE

Hendrix says that those with the gift of hope have the sure expectation in their hearts that rests solely on the promises of the Lord. Those with hope know what God has done for them and know His promises are true.

A person with the gift of hope really believes Romans 8:28 that all things work together for good to them that love God. They believe there are no "hopeless" situations.

Hendrix lists several characteristics of a person with the gift of hope:

- Sensitive and aware of spiritual concerns.
- Optimistic about other persons' motives and actions.
- Not easily disappointed in persons.
- Ability to "bounce back" from "hard knocks."
- Strong in difficult situations.
- Patient in time of trouble.

PRAYER

I want to make this very specific. The person who is gifted in prayer is an intercessor. An intercessor is someone greater than an ordinary prayer. These are people who are frequently asked, "Will you please pray for me?" because their friends know they communicate intensely with God.

All Christians should pray and must pray when they ask Jesus to come into their hearts and if they are to grow as Christians. However some Christians have the special ability and discipline to pray for extended periods of time on a regular basis and see frequent and specific answers to their prayers. They are prayer warriors. They have the gift of intercession.

HOSPITALITY

First Peter 4:9 in *The Message* says, "Be quick to give a meal to the hungry, a bed to the homeless—cheerfully." *The Amplified Bible* goes several steps further when it translates: "Be hospitable, that is, be a lover of strangers, with brotherly affection for the unknown guests, the foreigners, the poor and all others who come your way who are of Christ's body."

Flynn defines hospitality as the supernatural ability to provide open house and warm welcome for those in need of food and lodging.

Karen Mains explains there is a radical difference between entertaining and hospitality. In her book, *Open Heart—Open Home*, she says, "Entertaining is bondage. Its source is human pride. It seeks to impress. In contrast, hospitality is a freedom which liberates. Hospitality does not try to impress, but serves and ministers."

"Entertaining always puts 'things' before people," says Mains. "Hospitality puts people before things."

Entertaining is a talent. Hospitality is a gift.

Stop

Stop right here. The 12 gifts discussed so far are the ones this book will focus on. These 12 are: prophecy, service, teaching, exhorting, sharing, leading, mercy, love, enthusiasm, hope, prayer, and hospitality. They are the gifts in the instrument in chapter 4.

These 12 are "serving" gifts. You may be thinking, "Barbara, why did you leave out the other gifts?" Although others are mentioned, they are not primarily service-oriented. My emphasis is, without apology, on service since this book is written to help us understand, recognize, and develop those particular gifts.

The gift of wisdom is somewhat difficult to define. Many people, believers as well as nonbelievers, have wisdom. This is the kind of wisdom that comes from inherited intellect, experience, and hard study. But this is not the gift of wisdom described in James 1:5: "If any of you lacks wisdom, he should ask God, who gives generously to all without finding fault, and it will be given to him."

The gift of knowledge, according to some, enables believers to search and summarize the teachings in the Bible. Such scholars acquire deep insight into divine truth.

Every believer does not have the gift of faith, but every believer must have faith. By faith we receive our salvation and such faith is a gift of God (Eph. 2:8–9). Faith is necessary for our walk with God as well. But over and above this kind of faith is the gift given by the Holy Spirit to certain children of God.

Miracles, tongues, interpretation of tongues, and healings have been considered the "sign" gifts by many. In fact, certain scholars contend that sign gifts revealed God's presence to the world. Many have asked, "Were these gifts for the apostles only?" "Do we need these gifts since the Bible reveals the presence of God to us today?" Study for yourself and decide what you believe about these gifts.

The discerning of spirits is another gift mentioned by some. In the days of the New Testament, people were needed who could tell if a preacher was speaking under the impulse of the Holy Spirit, his own spirit, or an evil spirit. Today, we have the Bible. We can weigh what a preacher believes and teaches against what God's Word says.

The gift of apostleship is one that has been applied to missions. Many claim that they are one and the same. However, there are those who define the word *apostle* to mean those who were with Jesus and were eyewitnesses to the Resurrection. But Paul used the word *apostle* in a different sense to mean "sent one." Paul meant someone who had been sent for a specific ministry to a specific place. That sounds like a missionary to me.

I believe that every believer is to be a witness, but

certain believers have the gift of evangelism (Eph. 4:9). An evangelist has been described as a person with the ability to present the gospel message with exceptional clarity and an overwhelming burden.

Even if evangelism is not our gift, it is the privilege and responsibility of every believer to share the gospel. Some are gifted to be pastors. Pastoring is the special ability to assume a long-term responsibility for the spiritual welfare of a group of believers. Actually, the word *pastor* relates to sheep-raising. A pastor is a shepherd and is responsible for teaching, feeding, healing the wounds, and doing whatever else is necessary to see that they continue in the faith and grow in their spiritual lives.

So ends what was to have been a brief overview of the gifts of the Spirit. It is no easy task to set them down in understandable words. I pray that the Holy Spirit has been alongside helping you to understand as you have studied. For we need to know about these gifts and find our own so that we may use these gifts in service for Him.

The next step is to study ourselves. For we are a wondrous people—each a designer original.

---

[1]This was written in G. Campbell Morgan's foreword to a volume of poems entitled *Prairie Overcomer* by Edith Hickman Divall, published in 1906 by Three Hills in Alberta, Canada. Leslie Flynn used this quote by Morgan in his book *19 Gifts of the Spirit* (Wheaton, IL.: Victor Books, 1974), 30.

CHAPTER 3

ALL GOD'S CHILDREN ARE ORIGINALS

No two snowflakes are the same! Think of the trillions of snowflakes that make up just one beautiful snow flurry—and each crystal is different.

Should it be so hard to believe that each of us is unique, one-of-a-kind? We are original—right down to our finger-prints! The psalmist asked God, "Why do you bother with us? Why take a second look our way?" (Psalm 8:4 *The Message*).

Years after, Jesus gave the clearest answer: "And even the very hairs of your head are all numbered" (Matt. 10:30). That is meticulous creation, right down to the last strand!

I know God is awesome, but I've always believed that God had a cataclysmic interruption while He was counting the hairs on my head. My cat-fur fine and sparse locks could have used a few more clumps!

Nevertheless, my tresses are not like anybody else's on the face of the earth. I'm me. Each of us is different and unique.

You Are Original Because of Whose You Are

Each newborn baby resembles his or her parents in some ways yet differs in others. You inherit individual traits that make you different from any other person. Such traits include hair and eye color, body build, and many others. Since the genes for these traits came from your parents, you are like each parent in some ways. But since you received genes from both parents, you are not exactly like either one. Unless you have an identical twin, not one of the billions of people in the world is your genetic double. But even identical twins who are mirror images of each other and can be very much alike in mental and physical abilities and other traits are still different. Why? Read on.

You Are an Original Because of Where You Are

Environment has been defined as "all of the outside forces that act on an organism." Heredity determines the size to which your body will grow. However, factors in your environment, such as the foods you eat and the exercise you do, also affect your growth. Heredity controls what you can become. But what you do become often depends on environment. Home and family life, education, and friendships leave their marks on us. They make us unique.

You Are an Original Because of What You've Got

We are born with natural talents. These are often from or through our parents. So perhaps talents should be listed as part of heredity. However, environment plays a big part in our talents. Talents should be recognized, developed, and exercised.

In her book *Syllabus on Gifts*, Gladys Lewis lists 20 talents. She adds that the list could be inexhaustible, however, because natural or talent gifts are as numerous and diverse as people themselves:

Sports
Painting
Drawing
Sculpting
Carving
Sewing
Singing
Playing an instrument
Mechanical ability
Acting
Public speaking
Storytelling
Songwriting
Cooking
Social skills
Literary skills
Writing
Outdoor skills
Organizer of age groups
Construction skills

We have special skills and talents that are uniquely ours. Lewis explains that they may show up in work preference, hobbies, second jobs, or just daydreams. But talents are not spiritual gifts. Talents are given to every person, both Christians and non-Christians.

On the other hand, spiritual gifts are given to Christians only. "No unbeliever has one, and every true believer in Jesus does," says C. Peter Wagner, author of *Your Spiritual Gifts*. He adds that our spiritual gifts are not dedicated natural talents. God is able to take a natural talent in an unbeliever and transform it into a spiritual gift when that person gives her life to the Lord. But even in a case like that, the spiritual gift is much more than a souped-up natural talent. Both talents and spiritual gifts come from the Lord. But talents are natural gifts. Spiritual gifts are supernatural. Christians are to use their spiritual gifts and talents in service for others.

YOU ARE AN ORIGINAL BECAUSE OF HOW YOU ACT

"You've got personality..." the singer croons. And all of us do have "personality." James Birren defines personality as "the characteristic way we behave and respond to our environment."

One popular personality questionnaire deals with 16 personality factors:

> Reserved versus outgoing
> Low intelligence versus high intelligence
> Ego strength versus proneness to neuroticism
> Excitability versus insecurity
> Dominance versus submissiveness

Expedient versus conscientious
Timid versus uninhibited
Tough-minded versus tender-minded
Trusting versus suspicious
Practical versus imaginative
Unpretentious versus polished
Guilt proneness versus confidence
Radicalism versus conservatism
Self-sufficiency versus group dependency
High self-sentiment versus low self-sentiment
Relaxed versus tense

According to Birren in *Developmental Psychology*, personality is much more complicated than what is revealed on a 16-factor chart, however. Some additional dimensions of personality are self-concept, attitudes, goals and values, subjective feeling and perceptions, and life satisfaction and morale. Let's examine each of these briefly.

Self-concept: Awareness of self begins early when a child becomes aware of his body. Next comes a sense of self-identity, which leads to the development of self-esteem. Psychologists go into great detail with what happens or does not happen in the development of a good or bad image of self or what we think of ourselves. Many people, especially teenagers, do not like themselves. A person who does not like herself will often feel that others do not like her either. She will feel her gifts are not important and will be reluctant to use them in service for others.

Attitudes: Attitudes summarize a person's evaluation of specific objects, persons, or social issues. Attitudes that have received the most attention are conservatism/radicalism, tough-mindedness/tender-mindedness, and feelings toward other races and authoritarianism. Our attitudes reveal our beliefs. They plainly reveal the depth of our commitment to Christian ideals.

Goals and values: Our goals and values markedly influence our behavior. They are usually acquired during childhood from our families. Social class and ethnic background are also great influences.

Subjective feelings and perceptions: In easy-to-understand terms, this means how you feel about yourself and how you see other people. At different age levels, these feelings change.

Life satisfaction and morale: This factor deals with whether or not we consider ourselves to be happy. In childhood, happiness depends on acceptance from parents and peers and material surroundings. In adulthood, satisfaction is dependent on marriage, social status, and career advancement.

However, personality can and does change due to experiences and events. The biggest thing that can change our personalities is the biggest event in each of our lives: our salvation experience. We are motivated to share our faith and our gifts with others once we experience salvation ourselves.

YOU ARE AN ORIGINAL BECAUSE OF WHOSE YOU ARE: SECOND BIRTH

If that sounds familiar, it's because it is. We've talked about physical birth and parents and all they contribute to make you a designer original. Now let's consider your second birth. "I tell you the truth, unless a man is born again, he cannot see the Kingdom of God" Jesus informed a startled Nicodemus (John 3:3). And what an amazing new birth! The new birth is "God-begotten, not flesh-begotten, not sex-begotten" (John 1:13 *The Message*). John also announced the incredible news that this new birth gives us "the right to become children of God!" (John 1:12).

The most important experience any of us can have is the salvation experience. Accepting God's free gift of eternal life is life-changing. As we grow in the Lord, as we commit our lives to Him, our personalities change. The Holy Spirit comes into our lives at the point of new birth. He presents us with our birthday gift or gifts, our spiritual gifts. He begins to teach us about obedience, for only through obedience do we truly grow as Christians.

Paul said the Holy Spirit in our lives produces "affection for others, exuberance about life, serenity, a sense of compassion in the heart, and a conviction that a basic holiness permeates things and people. We find ourselves involved in loyal commitments, not needing to force our way in life, able to marshal and direct our energies wisely" (Gal. 5:22–23 *The Message*). This is the fruit of the Spirit, the evidence that He is in control of our lives.

Your wording of the fruit of the Spirit may be love, joy, peace, patience, kindness, goodness, faithfulness, humility, and self-control. Match this listing against the first listing. They are identical. They are the graces that prove we belong to the Lord. With the help of the Holy Spirit, they are attainable in our lives.

So the new birth brings amazing transformation. The Holy Spirit brings our spiritual gifts and walks alongside us to help us grow and develop our gifts and to grow and develop the fruit of the spirit.

Stuart Calvert cautions us about confusing the two in *Uniquely Gifted*. "Gifts," she explains, "define what a Christian does. Fruit defines who a Christian is."

It all spells out how precious we are to our Father. He

paid an awesome price for us to become His children. Author Dennis Guernsey makes it come alive when he says that "God loved me so much that He allowed His very own Son to die so that I might inherit eternal life. I must be of incredible worth to God." He adds, "Each of us must be of inestimable value to God. To diminish our value to Him is to diminish the meaning and value of Christ's death."

You are unique—an original. And you bring your one-of-a-kind personality, your precious redemption, as well as your spiritual gifts to life. And our Father wants it to be an abundant life used in service for Him.

Ready? Let's look for our gifts.

CHAPTER 4

ALL GOD'S CHILDREN SHOULD DISCOVER THEIR GIFTS

We must, as good stewards of our lives, discover, develop, and use our spiritual gifts. The following inventory was designed by John Hendrix and presented in his book *We Have These Treasures*. The inventory is based on Romans 12:3–13 and is designed to do two things: (1) it should help us understand more about our spiritual gifts; (2) it should provide us with a profile of our leadership characteristics.[1]

The inventory consists of 60 items. Some items reflect concrete actions; other items are descriptive of traits; and still others are statements of belief or value.

Directions: As you read each item, decide whether the sentence is true or descriptive of you. Circle the letter to the right of the sentence that most accurately reflects your decision. Your first response to the question is usually the best.

N—Not at all, this is untrue for me.

O—Occasionally, this is true for me about 25 percent of the time.

F—Frequently, this describes me about 50 percent of the time.

M—Most of the time this would describe me.

H—Highly characteristic, this is definitely true for me.

1. I'm not afraid to speak for the truth.   N O F M H

2. In helping people, I seem to know the right thing to do.   N O F M H

3. I enjoy discussing ideas and issues.   N O F M H

4. Others seem to look to me for advice and help.   N O F M H

5. I like to keep my life simple and natural. N O F M H

6. Setting and achieving goals is important to me.   N O F M H

7. Doing things for people in need makes me happy.   N O F M H

8. I can give to others without expecting anything in return.   N O F M H

9. I get excited about my faith. N O F M H

10. I am an optimistic, positive person. N O F M H

11. I am aware of the miraculous aspects
of life. N O F M H

12. I enjoy making people feel at home. N O F M H

13. Expressing my feelings is easy for me. N O F M H

14. I'm concerned that people don't grow
more as Christians. N O F M H

15. I am never bored. N O F M H

16. I am accepting of others' faults and
failures. N O F M H

17. I find strength from bearing others'
burdens. N O F M H

18. Accomplishing something worthwhile
takes great effort. N O F M H

19. It's not important for others to know the
good things I do. N O F M H

20. I enjoy sharing what I have with others. N O F M H

21. Problems are a challenge to me. N O F M H

22. Injustice and evil in the world trouble me. N O F M H

23. I find prayer to be a great source of strength. N O F M H

24. I like to help people without being asked. N O F M H

25. Stating the facts in a situation is something I do well. N O F M H

26. I can usually encourage people to do things. N O F M H

27. I look for ways to get acquainted with new friends. N O F M H

28. I like to see all the pieces of a problem come together. N O F M H

29. I am attracted to people who are hurting. N O F M H

30. I don't hold grudges against people. N O F M H

31. I am eager to see good things happen to people. N O F M H

32. Things eventually work out for the good. N O F M H

33. Talking to God is easy for me. N O F M H

34. I never meet a stranger. N O F M H

35. What I have to say is usually helpful to people. N O F M H

36. Difficult situations bring out the best in me. N O F M H

37. Every day is new for me.   N O F M H

38. I'm not afraid to be warm and close
to people.   N O F M H

39. I like to work with sick and neglected
people.   N O F M H

40. I consider myself to be a hard worker.   N O F M H

41. I have an urge to tell others about my
life in Christ.   N O F M H

42. I'm a good counselor.   N O F M H

43. I can usually think clearly in confusion.   N O F M H

44. I enjoy doing little things to help people.   N O F M H

45. I will stand alone on something I believe
in strongly.   N O F M H

46. I don't care who gets credit for a job
well done.   N O F M H

47. I like to tell people what's important
to me.   N O F M H

48. My life is an open book for others to see.   N O F M H

49. Completing a job is important to me.   N O F M H

50. I somehow know how people in distress
feel.   N O F M H

51. I feel kinship with most people I meet.　N O F M H

52. I usually have energy to burn.　N O F M H

53. I am not easily disappointed.　N O F M H

54. I pray every day.　N O F M H

55. My home is open to lots of people.　N O F M H

56. People see me as a frank and outspoken
person.　N O F M H

57. I will tell people if I think they're doing
wrong.　N O F M H

58. Possessions are meant to be shared.　N O F M H

59. I'd rather do something myself than get
others to do it.　N O F M H

60. I have confidence in things I cannot see. N O F M H

SCORE SHEET

Instructions: Transfer your letter responses from the inventory to each of the 12 scales below and write in the value for each response.

N = -2
O = -1   Sum up the values of items in each scale for a score.
F = 0
M = +1
H = +2

I. PROPHECY

Item	I	22	35	45	56
Letter					
Value					

Score

2. SERVICE

Item	2	24	44	46	59
Letter					
Value					

Score

3. TEACHING

Item	3	21	25	43	47
Letter					
Value					

Score

4. EXHORTING

Item	4	14	26	42	57
Letter					
Value					

Score

5. SHARING

Item	5	19	41	48	58
Letter					
Value					

Score

6. LEADING

Item	6	18	28	40	49
Letter					
Value					

Score

7. MERCY

Item	7	17	29	39	50
Letter					
Value					

Score

8. LOVE

Item	8	16	30	38	51
Letter					
Value					

Score

9. ENTHUSIASM

Item	9	15	31	37	52
Letter					
Value					

Score

10. HOPE

Item	10	32	36	53	60
Letter					
Value					

Score

11. PRAYER

Item	11	13	23	33	54
Letter					
Value					

Score

12. HOSPITALITY

Item	12	20	27	34	55
Letter					
Value					

Score

PROFILE A

Directions: Enter your total score for each scale in the box provided, and then chart each score at the appropriate point on the graph.

SCALE   SCORE

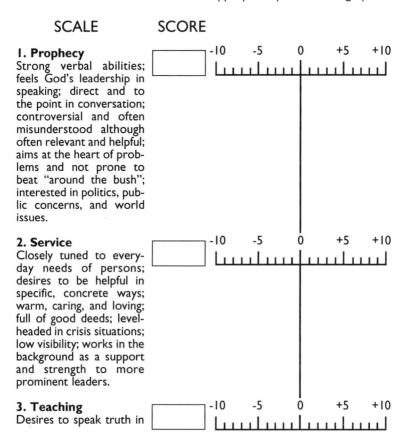

1. Prophecy
Strong verbal abilities; feels God's leadership in speaking; direct and to the point in conversation; controversial and often misunderstood although often relevant and helpful; aims at the heart of problems and not prone to beat "around the bush"; interested in politics, public concerns, and world issues.

2. Service
Closely tuned to everyday needs of persons; desires to be helpful in specific, concrete ways; warm, caring, and loving; full of good deeds; level-headed in crisis situations; low visibility; works in the background as a support and strength to more prominent leaders.

3. Teaching
Desires to speak truth in

ways that nurture growth; capacity to analyze, explain, and interpret facts; levelheaded; ability to focus on problems and issues; willingness to "be an example" for others.

4. Exhorting
Capacity for stirring and inspiring speech; sensitive to others' problems and dilemmas; provides revealing answers that others find helpful; confrontational, but not offensive; long-suffering and patient with the weakness of others.

5. Sharing
Appreciation for simple and natural things; willing to share material possessions; open in sharing personal experience particularly in relation to one's faith; in touch with inner feelings and an ability to communicate these feelings to others; satisfaction from sharing one's resources freely.

6. Leading
Interested in organization and delegation; confident in "standing before" others; ability to see needs; hardworking; giving attention to detail; concerned about directions that are according to the purposes and the will of God.

7. Mercy
Compassionate and caring; bearing others' burdens; sensing in others the emotions of pain,

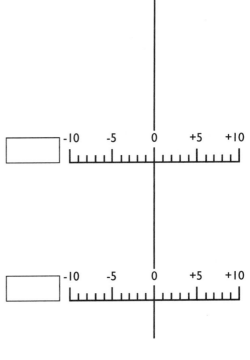

affliction, and despair; action-oriented; a readiness of mind to help those who are weak; a feeling of happiness that comes from doing merciful deeds.

8. Love
Capacity for intimacy and closeness; feelings of affection toward many people; a desire to be in harmony with others; ability to give without expectation of return; orientation to practical needs of others; a belief that people are "one big family."

9. Enthusiasm
Highly motivated; ability to bring "sparkle" and excitement to a situation; unusual capacity to be caught up and absorbed in a task; intense and emotional; feeling of adventure about past, present, and future events.

10. Hope
Sensitive and aware of spiritual concerns; optimistic about other persons' motives and actions; not easily disappointed in persons; ability to "bounce back" from "hard knocks"; strong in difficult situations; patient in time of trouble.

11. Prayer
Capacity to express affection and love in simple ways; childlike, playful, and spontaneous; lacking in self-consciousness;

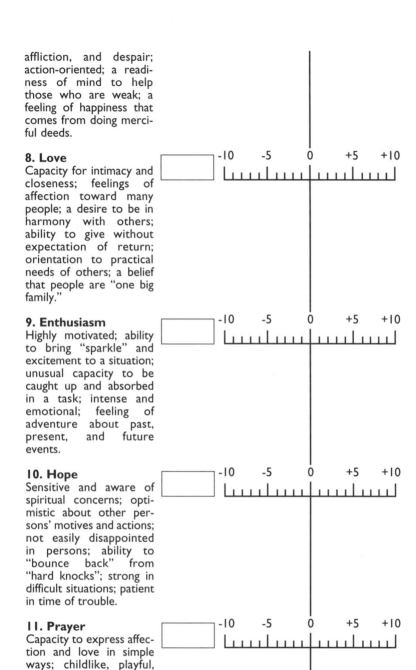

-10   -5   0   +5   +10

-10   -5   0   +5   +10

-10   -5   0   +5   +10

-10   -5   0   +5   +10

ability to put into words what the "heart" is saying.

12. Hospitality
Outgoing, informal, and friendly; a "welcoming" attitude to friends and strangers alike; ability to help others feel "at home" in all kinds of situations; desire to do things for others with no thought of return; willingness to be helpful without being asked.

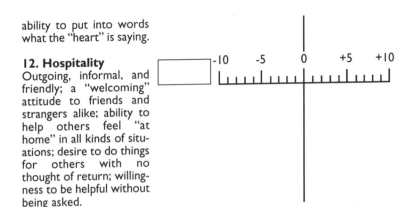

-10   -5   0   +5   +10

SUMMARY PROFILE B

Directions: *Total* scores according to the three categories and plot your three totals on the profile triangle. Any negative score should be plotted at zero. Connect with three lines and shade in. It will look something like this:

(but different)

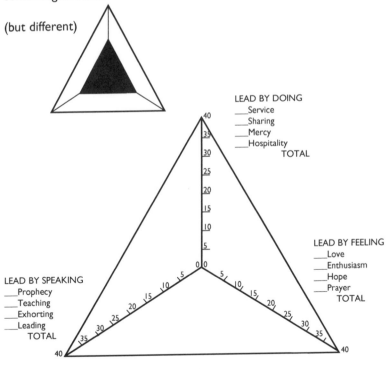

LEAD BY DOING
___Service
___Sharing
___Mercy
___Hospitality
                TOTAL

LEAD BY FEELING
___Love
___Enthusiasm
___Hope
___Prayer
                TOTAL

LEAD BY SPEAKING
___Prophecy
___Teaching
___Exhorting
___Leading
                TOTAL

INTERPRETING MY GIFTS WORK SHEET

1. The three gifts I score highest in are (see Profile A):

   _____

   _____

   _____

2. Some personal characteristics (traits, abilities, beliefs) that help me see my gifts are (see Profile A):

   _____

   _____

   _____

3. Some Bible passages that help me understand my gifts are:

   _____

   _____

4. In general, my leadership style seems to be (choose from Lead by Doing, Lead by Speaking, Lead by Feeling in Summary Profile B):

   _____

5. I see my gifts best suited to the following church jobs and tasks:

   _____

   _____

   _____

6. My gifts may be leading me into a church-related vocation__ yes __perhaps __no

At this point you may feel overwhelmed with all the testing. Hang in there; the next chapter will give us some answers to your scores. And all God's children need answers!

---
¹John D. Hendrix, *We Have These Treasures* (Nashville: Convention Press, 1979), 22–28. All rights reserved. Used by permission.

CHAPTER 5

ALL GOD'S CHILDREN NEED ANSWERS

I remember quite vividly when I took the inventory you have just taken. I thought I had been taken! I discovered, to my horror, that I had no mercy and only a smidgen of a sign of the gift of hospitality. This test had to be wrong! I had just led a retreat conference on "Using the Home as a Base for Witness." The Joiner residence is known as the "open house" of Columbiana, Alabama. International students have prepared a million dishes in my kitchen. Missionaries spend weeks with us when visiting in our area. Teenagers have prayed thousands of prayers on my living room floor at their weekly missions meetings. *I have the gift of hospitality!*

The first thing I did was check all my "low" scores. (You, too?) I was the typical furious "foot" and enraged "ear" Paul talked about in 1 Corinthians 12:15,16. I wanted all the gifts.

It was not important to me to look for evidences of what my gifts could be. A friend had to say to me, "Your gifts are in speaking, aren't they?" before I even considered them at all.

Let us proceed to look realistically at what your inventory revealed and what it could mean in your life.

1. Don't despair over low scores. Tests are not infallible. Remember in school when you were having a bad day and a test score reflected that? This test may not be true for you.

However, if the test is fairly accurate, your low score in a certain area does not mean you cannot and should not do that particular activity ever again. A good example of this is sharing or giving. Let's say your score in sharing says that giving is not your gift. It isn't mine either. I have already blamed this weakness of mine on my "depression" parents and their frugal Scottish ancestors. Although my gift is not giving, as a Christian I'm still required to be found faithful, to tithe at the very least. I also delight in giving sacrificially to missions offerings. And since I was a young girl I've been taught to be a good steward of my time, money, and personality. No doubt about it, I'm to be a faithful giver even if I'm not a gifted giver.

Another good example is hospitality. So I don't have the gift of hospitality. When I've compared myself to some of the hospitable women in chapter 7, I can recognize my failings clearly. The Lord knew I'd travel a great deal (exercising my gift of speaking and teaching missions every chance I get!). I also have a husband who goes to bed before 10:00 P.M. no matter how special a guest might be. I've been tempted to call him the same name that Mary Lou Levrets, retired missionary to Ibadan, Nigeria, calls her husband, Fred. She calls him Morning Glory because he closes up at night!

Let me quickly add that both Mary Lou and Fred practice warm, wonderful hospitality. I enjoyed immensely the time I spent in their home in Ibadan. I'll never forget the exciting trip up country to Kaduna, Nigeria, where they transformed their little Peugeot into a tour bus, a picnic pavilion, and a good place for friendship to grow.

A word in defense of Homer, my Morning Glory: He has patiently endured my penchant for people for all the years of our married life, and has been my number one helper and supporter. So what if he does retire early? He does have to rise and shine at 5:00 A.M. each morning.

Read Romans 12:13. We are not excused from practicing hospitality. Christians are commanded to be hospitable. Women have often been taught that opening their homes is a way of opening their hearts. Our homes have traditionally been our ministry and missions headquarters.

2. Don't despair over total minus scores. Hendrix says that it is possible that Summary Profile B will produce total minus scores, therefore, nothing will show on the profile triangle. "If that happens," says Hendrix, "go back to Profile Sheet A and concentrate on individual gifts."

Hendrix adds that minus scores should not be interpreted in a negative manner, as an absence of gifts. Any total score that does not show on the profile triangle should be considered as "average." The important principle to remember is to measure on strengths whether in individual gifts or total groupings of gifts.

3. Look instead at the gifts where you score highest. Turn back to the Interpreting My Gifts Work Sheet. Which gifts did you place after question 1? Were you surprised? If you reacted as I did, you were not really surprised. Speaking has always been my "thing." As a little girl I loved telling stories. Required oratorical contests in school were fun for me. I was always entered in contests and won enough to keep hope alive!

When I graduated from high school my father rejected the field of medicine as a career for me. I know now that if I had really wanted to be a doctor, I would have found a way! At this point, I turned to the natural talent I had (I knew very little about spiritual gifts as a high school senior) and I chose to go for a degree in public speaking. I discovered debate and loved it. All this time I was using what I thought was my natural talent to teach children in Sunday School and to speak at meetings, retreats, and conventions. The truth of the matter is that God has chosen to gift me in the area of my natural talents. As I developed my abilities in speaking, I was developing and using my spiritual gifts.

How clearly I can see the differences in the two now. Perhaps the best way to show the difference is to tell you about a missions convention for teenagers in Oklahoma. I had agreed to be the theme speaker for the state meeting. A week before the meeting, I caught a really nasty cold (I thought). As my time of departure came nearer, it grew worse. Finally, the night before I was to fly to Oklahoma City, my husband dragged my feverish body to the clinic.

"Flu!" pronounced the doctor. "What hospital do you want?"

"None," I croaked. "I have a meeting this weekend."

"Ha!" shouted my husband and the doctor simultaneously.

"But you don't understand. I'm speaking three times and leading a conference."

They looked at me in disbelief, but I held my ground.

"Give me a shot and some medicine that won't make me

crazy. I'll be fine," I assured them.

The next morning my husband took me to the airport, muttering all the way. He was doing the muttering; I was nearly comatose. God had Sheryl Churchill, a friend from Birmingham, on my same flight to Texas! Homer gratefully turned me over to her, and made her promise to get me on the correct flight to Oklahoma City. Sheryl somehow buckled my sagging body into the seat next to hers. She says I told her some interesting things on that flight. She didn't hear them all because she was trying to shield herself from all my germs!

When we reached the Dallas/Fort Worth airport, Sheryl tells me she led me to my flight, begged the flight attendant to turn me over personally to the friend who was meeting me in Oklahoma City, and fled to disinfect herself!

I don't remember that flight or my trip by car to Oklahoma Baptist University. I do remember staggering into the convention director's room to announce my arrival. Her scream, "You're sick!" pierced my foggy brain.

"But I'm here," I managed feebly.

Before I speak I've always prayed that I would get out of the way so God could have control. I've always meant that prayer, but this time I was totally in earnest. I had no control. As I rose to speak that night, the room spun dizzily around me. I thought, "I'll never make it to the podium." Once there, holding on tightly to steady the world, I thought, "I won't know what I am saying!"

In addition, my head was full of cotton and my teeth felt like they had little sweaters on them. But I took a deep breath and God began to speak to those teenagers.

You want to know how I know God was speaking to them? The answer is simple. Once in awhile a group like this will give a speaker a standing ovation. If I ever get one, it's usually at the end of a meeting after I've spoken several times (maybe it's because it is the last time!). But that night in Shawnee, Oklahoma, after I spoke at the first session, the girls stood and clapped and clapped. I took the applause, still holding on tightly, with great humility. I knew beyond a shadow of a doubt Who had spoken that night.

The next morning the medicine had done its work and I was much better. I "helped" the Lord from there on out. And there were no more standing ovations! You know, the Lord can do fine—if we'll let Him.

The difference between the talent and the gift should be His supernatural control—if we'll let Him. That doesn't mean we don't have to work, to plan, and to prepare. He works best through us when we have worked, planned, and prepared. But the final step should always be committing it to Him.

4. Look at your highest scores. Turn back to chapter 2 for a fuller definition of each one. Mark the passages concerning your possible gifts. Mark the traits, abilities, and beliefs you find in those definitions. Also look back at the score sheet in chapter 4. For example, if you scored high in "Sharing," check back on questions 5, 19, 41, 48, and 58. Also check profile A for its short definition of your possible gifts.

5. Check your Bible for more explanation. Some major gift passages are Romans 12:6–13; 1 Corinthians 12–14; and Ephesians 4. Read these passages in several translations. In addition, use the concordance in your Bible and look for passages on sharing or giving or whatever your gift could be.

6. *Examine your answers on questions 4 and 5 on the Interpreting My Gifts Work Sheet.* Hendrix attempts to make this easier for us by giving some suggestions of ways we use gifts in the three categories he has identified.

Leading by Doing (service, sharing, hospitality, mercy)
Building and equipment
Finances and budget
Food preparation
Fellowships
Deacon
Usher
Witnessing and outreach
Stewardship
Hospital ministry
Visitation
Missions
Social ministries

Leading by Speaking (prophecy, teaching, exhorting, leading)
Pastor
Teaching
Music
Group leader
Minister of education
Evangelism and witnessing
Leader training
Committee chairperson
Devotionals
Radio and television
Moral concerns
Social ministries
Public relations

Leading by Feeling (prayer, hope, love, enthusiasm)
Counseling
Recreation and sports
Youth ministry
Day care
Kindergarten
Spiritual discipline (Bible study, prayer)
Revivals
Renewal
Prayer groups
Family ministry

7. God may have gifted you for some of these ministries. He may also have gifted you for other ministries that are not listed here. This is just the tip of the iceberg as far as the work He planned for us.

If there were room in this book, there would be another chapter which would deal with the fact that God does the gifting, but many women do not use the gifts God has given them. They are content to sit back and waste their gifts. Each woman, in light of her commitment and gifts, should ask, "How can I use my gifts to share the love of Christ?"

8. Sometimes friends see your gifts more clearly than you do. Remember somebody had to say to me, "Your gifts are in speaking, aren't they?" before I'd even look at my strengths? Right now, share your inventory scores with a friend—one who knows you well. Discuss your score sheets together. Affirm each other.

In the last 12 years, I've taught this book hundreds of times. After taking the test, people have literally descended on me with comments and questions. After teaching several hundred young people in an overnight session, one teenager ran up to me and shouted, "I have the gift of extortion!"

"No," I laughed. "You have the gift of exhortation!"

"What in the world is that?" she asked.

"That means you are an encourager, you tell people that they can do it! You tell them that you believe in them. They come to you for advice."

"That's me!" she crowed. "My friends never make a move without checking with me first!"

Her friends had already affirmed her gift.

I enjoy hearing dialogue between friends after testing. "Well, of course you have the gift of mercy. It's plain to see."

"All of us enjoy your gift of hospitality."

"You are a prayer warrior."

The first time I led an all-day, covered-dish study, a pure bundle of energy scuddled down the aisle before the meeting started. She looked me in the eye and announced: "I'm 82, and it's about time somebody came to help me find my spiritual gifts."

After taking the test, she bounded up to me and declared, "I didn't need this test to tell me I'm a prayer warrior! Honey, I have prayer journals dating back to World War I. I know how to go to the throne of God! But I never knew I had the gift of teaching..." She leaned close to me and confided, "I only finished the sixth grade. We lived way out in the country. And now I've found out I have the gift of teaching! I've already gone to a children's worker who is here today. She said last week that she had more than 30 children in her group and no helper. I told her I'd be there Wednesday night. I also told her that I've never taught before, but I'm a gifted teacher and she's lucky to have me!"

I love that spirit and would love to be in that class.

9. Go to work. Begin using your gifts as soon as you can. Search out opportunities. Look at opportunities that are yours right now.

Author Jo Berry says to use trial and error as a process of discovery. She adds, "The Lord doesn't strike us dead for exploring possibilities. He rewards pure motives and honest efforts."

But do use your gifts. Use is the key. Ask yourself, "How can I use my gifts?" Then find ways you can use your gifts in ministry with others. For example, do you have the gift of hospitality? Use that gift to throw a party for some disabled children in your community. Do you have the gift of teaching? Use that gift to teach an international to read.

Do you get the picture? Remember that use is the key. Our gifts are given to us for a purpose. God gave us our gifts to give to others. They are yours for the giving.

CHAPTER 6

ALL GOD'S CHILDREN OUGHT TO SERVE

Every passage on gifts in the Bible is accompanied by directions for use. John Hendrix says that's because gifts and discipleship go together like jelly and peanut butter. "They fit," he claims.

Paul said they fit every time he talked about gifts. In Ephesians 4:12 he explained that gifts are given "to prepare God's people for works of service, so that the body of Christ may be built up." In speaking to the Corinthian church Paul said, "Now to each one the manifestation of the Spirit is given for the common good (1 Cor. 12:7). Paul urged the Christians at Rome: "We have different gifts, according to the grace given us" (Rom. 12:6).

Perhaps a verse in 1 Peter says it best: "Each one should use whatever gift he has received to serve others" (1 Peter 4:10). A high school senior also said it well: "God has given me abilities and powers to develop in the best way I can. He created me for a purpose. He gave me life and through service to Him I return both life and talents."

Like that high school senior, it is my desire to return my life and my gifts and talents to the Lord. The way God has led me to do this is through investing my time and energies with teenaged girls. They are my joy as well as my training ground, and sometimes my battleground!

I pour my gifts of teaching and leading into these girls and bathe all of it with my third gift of prayer.

My best friend, Stuart Calvert, and I don't always see eye-to-eye on spiritual gifts. But she knows gifts. Read her gem of a book, *Uniquely Gifted*. She also knows me. In her book she says: "The experiences of my friend Barbara Joiner inspire me to pray more specifically, and to give more generously to missions. Her stories weave my emotions like a French braid, or maybe pigtail plaits. She teaches through laughter and through tears. "Pizzazzy" state youth missions conventions prove her ability to incorporate the gifts of many people. A variety of missions trips prove her ability to organize toward worthwhile goals, to insist the team members reach and even stretch their potential, and to guide by example. As a result of her leadership gift, young ladies involved become flexible and remain unflappable, regardless of the conditions that greet them."

Well—I'm not sure I'm that woman, but as Popeye would say, "I yam what I yam." And whatever I yam, I want to be used by the Lord.

All of us need to find channels for our gifts. Let's look at the list of gifts Hendrix uses in his inventory and search for how these gifts can be used in missions, ministry, and discipleship to develop and use each God-given gift.

1. Prophecy. Opportunities in missions and ministry can be great shapers of ideas. Some with the gift of prophecy learn to use it effectively by experiencing things that affect their lives and the lives of others. They learn to speak out against injustice. Some will begin to speak with eloquence because God has gifted them with the gift of prophecy.

2. Service. Ministry organizations and planned group activities are often very service oriented. These activities can help people with the gift of service best utilize their gift.

Active involvement in community ministries is particularly important for those with this gift. They are effective in establishing day-care centers or food pantries for those in need, providing tutors for inner-city schools, or working with and in nearby nursing homes. Churches and ministries need to attract such women. But even more important, participating in ministry gives those women a chance to recognize, develop, and use their gift of service.

3. Teaching. Sunday School and Bible studies give many women the opportunity to use their gift of teaching. Good teachers for particular age levels are always in demand.
In addition, through ministry other teaching opportunities arise. Tutoring, teaching literacy classes, teaching sign language, and teaching English as a second language all call out the best we have to give.

4. Exhorting. (It's perfectly legal to look back in chaps. 2 and 4 for definitions whenever you need to do so!) The first example that comes to mind in exhortation is the camping experience of my oldest daughter, Jackie. For two summers Jackie was a camp counselor at Lake Sallateeska, a Christian camp in Illinois. I don't know how much good

Jackie did for the young campers there, but I could see what camp did for her.

Jackie had to learn to counsel, to listen, and to comfort when homesickness hit. She had to solve problems (some of her own making!). Sensitivity to others became a character trait, a grace that was added to her lifestyle.

Not all teenaged girls have the opportunity to serve for a whole summer, but church-sponsored day camping offers similar experiences. Vacation Bible School does as well. Such opportunities are open for women as well as teenagers.

5. Sharing. My mother always said, "It's not what you would do with the $1 million you don't have, it's what you are doing with the quarter you've got in your pocket." It's fun to encourage others to give their quarters joyfully. That's the beginning of sacrificial giving and good stewardship.

Sharing time can be even harder. The world is greedy for our time. It's difficult teaching and learning that all of our time belongs to God. Richard Foster shares a very human experience in his book *Celebration of Discipline.* "As I was in the frantic final throes of writing my doctoral dissertation I received a phone call from a friend. His wife had taken the car and he wondered if I could take him on a number of errands. Trapped, I consented, inwardly cursing my luck. As I ran out the door I grabbed Bonhoeffer's *Life Together*, thinking that I might have an opportunity to read in it. Through each errand I inwardly fretted and fumed at the loss of precious time. Finally, at a supermarket, the final stop, I waved my friend on saying I would wait in the car. I picked up my book, opened it to the marker and read these words: 'The second service that one should perform for another in a Christian community is that of active helpfulness. This means, initially, simple assistance in trifling, external matters. There is a multitude of these things wherever people live together. Nobody is too good for the meanest service. One who worries about the loss of time that such petty, outward acts of helpfulness entail is usually taking the importance of his own career too solemnly.'"

After typing these words from Bonhoeffer I closed my typewriter and did some simple assisting that I had been putting off!

6. Leading. Nowhere in the church does a woman have better opportunities to discover, develop, and use her gift of leadership than in women's organizations. And a multitude of other leadership positions exist in the local church from leading adult groups to the even more important jobs of leading youth and children (you can tell where my sentiments lie!). If a woman's gift is leadership, she will respond to such challenges. Many of us learn to lead adequately even if leadership is not our gift.

Youth also need opportunities to lead. Several summers ago, nine of us served on a missions team—seven girls and two adults. Three senior girls—all strong leaders, were on the team. They were all seasoned missions veterans with three years of experience working in Taos, New Mexico. These three seniors led our three small teams in Massachusetts. They planned each day's activities, made assignments, and were responsible for record keeping and all the nitty-gritty details of materials and refreshments. The other adult and I were in small groups; we followed "orders."

I'm here to testify that our team leaders did an outstanding job. I suspect Tracy, Mandy, and Donnalee may someday rule the world! Those with this gift need a chance to lead.

7. Mercy. Compassion and caring should be the reaction of Christians to human needs. As we are faced with needs, we soon discover if we are gifted with mercy. Even if mercy is not our gift, we should still practice mercy or we don't deserve the name of our Lord. Ministry should put us in touch with people who need physical, mental, and spiritual help.

Thirty years of working with young people in migrant camps have taught me much about mercy. I, along with many young women and young men, have learned that loving migrants is loving the Father.

8. Love. Ray Stedman in his book *Body Life* explains: "Christ loves this world and the men and women in it. He loves the homeless, pathetic derelicts who drift up and down the streets of our big cities in increasing numbers. He loves the narcotics victims, the alcoholics, the devotees of sex perversions, the acid heads and prostitutes. He loves the hard-driving, hard-headed businessmen who have made a god of success and have fallen for the illusion that wealth means happiness. He loves them all and wants to reach them—through His body. That's why He equipped it with gifts, and filled it with His life."

He wants to fill it with His love, too. Jack MacGorman, author of *The Gifts of the Spirit*, has said bluntly that love is the indispensable medium for the exercise of all gifts. "Without love," he declares, "none of the spiritual gifts can function."

Galatians 5:13 admonishes, "Serve one another in love." Love has plenty of room to develop and be shared as we serve.

9. Enthusiasm. Many girls are crazy about adventure. They can be so excited about what they're doing—if they are in on the planning and putting together of the programs, the projects, the dinners, or parties. It's amazing what girls and their leaders can do together.

The same principles hold true for women, too. Try something new. It might even work.

Joy Steincross, a fellow youth leader and friend, told me that when she was a teenager she tried participating in many organizations. "But," she confided, "missions was my thing. Missions turned me on." That was some "turn on." Each of us needs to discover what we are most enthusiastic about. Joy found her gift in missions. She lights up a room!

10. Hope. Sensitivity and awareness, key ingredients of hope, bloom in mission settings. In a world beset with "me-ism," with selfishness, with "I'm worth it" philosophy, missions is a fresh wind blowing. Look at the hunger, look at the poverty, look at the hopeless, look at the lost. What can I do to help?

One of the precious moments at migrant camp one summer showed the joy of hope. My daughter Jennifer had finished finals at Auburn University and rushed straight to south Alabama to be part of our church's migrant ministry. She hadn't missed in 16 years since she went with her mother (me) when she was only four years old.

That first year Jen went to migrant camp, she and Lydia Garcia (also four) became fast friends. Every year the little blonde-haired Anglo could hardly wait to see her little black-haired Mexican American friend. But the year Lydia turned eight, the Garcias joined the Sugar Beet Trail out in the West. Jen was heartbroken. Eight-year-olds don't keep in touch with each other, especially when one is on the migrant trail.

We believe there are three good things we try to share with migrants: (1) the Lord, (2) our friendship, (3) hope of getting off the migrant trail. That last one is accomplished usually in one of two ways—death or education.

That summer at migrant camp Jennifer got word from Lydia for the first time in years. She shared that news with all of us with tears flowing freely. "Lydia is going to college! My friend is going to college—just like I am!"

Hope never dies once it is allowed to bloom.

11. Prayer. Women have been effective in engaging in ministry and personal witnessing because of the prayer that has undergirded these efforts. Prayer warriors are empowering.

I've been nurtured personally by prayer retreats. I've been challenged to pray daily for missionaries. I've become disciplined to pray for missions needs. But the best prayer times for me are the wonderful, refreshing, soul-searching prayer circles with youth. Nothing is quite as exciting as seeing God contacted on a one-to-one basis for the very first time. I'll never forget Alison's first words to the Father. Three times she had attended a missions meeting. She had never been to a missions meeting before in her life. When she moved to Columbiana, the girls took her in, accepted her, loved her.

At Alison's third meeting, we ended as usual with the prayer circle. Each girl thanked God for Alison. When the girl next to Alison finished her prayer, Alison blurted out her first prayer of thanks to the Lord. It was simple. There was no formal address, just six heartfelt words: "I'm so glad somebody likes me."

It wasn't long before Alison realized God loves her. Our group rejoiced as she accepted Christ as her Savior. Oh, yes, we have learned about prayer. Some of those girls may have found their gift; all of us have learned to speak with the heart.

12. Hospitality. I've already discussed the "open-door" policy of Christian women in chapter 2. I think teenagers and children learn by example. As I host our youth meetings, the girls see and feel they are welcome in my home. It is not always practical for groups from church to meet in homes. Make a way to do this, however, on special occasions. This gift is needed in our impersonal world.

We naturally think of inviting our friends and fellow Christians into our homes. But what about using your gift of hospitality to reach non-Christians? For example, international students you meet could be invited to your home for a holiday meal.

Obviously, I think women's organizations offer a nurturing place and a using place for our gifts. This is absolutely crucial. We must use the gifts God has given us.

William McRae reminds us that if we fail to contribute our gifts to the body of Christ, and if we fail to function in the capacity for which we have been equipped, the body will be impoverished. That means the body will be hurt, injured, hungry. He states, "We have been given our capacities for their profit. Nothing but immoral selfishness withholds that which has been designed and provided by our Lord for the profit of others."

Jo Berry, author of *The Priscilla Principle,* reminds us that God gifted us for service, not to make us look good. Your gifts are not for you to "glory in," but for the glory of God. He has entrusted them to you. They are yours for the giving.

CHAPTER 7

ALL GOD'S CHILDREN NEED A PARAGON

A paragon is neither a many-sided geometric figure, nor something you put in your bathwater to "take you away." It is, according to Merriam-Webster, a model or pattern of excellence. So this chapter will present to you gifted paragons from Bible times and from today. But we want to go beyond paragon to people you know. For God did not gift exceptional Christians. He gifted us all.

I owe special thanks to a dozen friends for telling me whom they consider gifted prophets and servants and on down the list. But my friends did not perform as I expected. I thought there would be a clear pattern. I expected they would pick an outstanding woman as a modern-day prophet, for example. They did not agree. There were instances where as many as four would name the same woman as gifted in the same category, but no star shone over one woman as *the* gifted one.

Each of our gifts is important, and many women have used their gifts to touch others' lives. As you read these examples, think about the women you know who are using their gifts. Then consider how you can use your gifts.

1. Prophecy

During Bible days, before the revelation of Jesus had been made known, prophecy meant a direct revelation from God. And women prophesied.

Exodus 15:20 calls Miriam, the sister of Moses and Aaron, a prophetess. Judges 4:4 names Deborah not only a prophetess, but also a judge. Chapters 4 and 5 also identify Deborah as a military leader and heroine. Aided by Barak, she rallied the tribes of Israel to defeat the Canaanites.

During the reign of Josiah when the scroll was found in the temple, Josiah immediately sent the scroll to Huldah, a prophetess (2 Kings 22:14).

In New Testament times, there was Anna who recognized the baby Jesus as the Messiah (Luke 2:36–38). Acts 21:9 mentions the four daughters of Philip the evangelist who were all prophetesses.

Joel in Old Testament times had said, "Your sons and daughters will prophesy" (Joel 2:28).

Modern-day prophets make the Scripture clear and relate it to life. They speak the truth boldly with integrity. Anne Graham Lotz, the daughter of famed evangelist Billy Graham, is such a woman. I remember the first time I heard Anne speak. I was electrified! She didn't speak; she preached! She did so with great clarity and power. Each time I've heard her since, my conviction has been verified. Her father's mantle has fallen on her. More specifically, God has gifted her with prophecy.

Another young woman who has blazed into our hearing is Beth Moore from Houston, Texas. Her books have become best-sellers. Thousands of women have been involved in her study courses. But Beth on video, and even more so in person, has captivated women everywhere. She is being used of God as an incomparable prophet.

One more example: Rebecca Vincent (now Hollis) is an extraordinary young woman. On our first mission trip to Jamaica, we were partners teaching 11- and 12-year-olds. The first day, we had 81 (and it grew daily!). They tapped every gift we had and God lent us a few we desperately needed.

The second day of Bible School, Rebecca taught the Bible lesson about Elijah and the prophets of Baal. She laid the wood on the altar (figuratively) and then she widened those children's eyes as she called out the pleas of those false prophets to their gods.

"What a teacher!" I marveled. And then she spun the story of Elijah. She made those buckets of water so real that the children drew their feet away from the imaginary altar. Spellbound, they heard her tell of Elijah calling on the one true God. When the wood blazed into fire, they shielded their faces from the inferno.

Then Rebecca leaned forward toward the children and confided, "If God can set on fire that soggy wood, just imagine what a blaze He can start in your heart!"

Then she preached to them the wonderful plan God has for us all!

On the trip home I said to Rebecca, "Girl, you have the gift of prophecy!" Sure enough, when I wrote this book, I could hardly wait for Rebecca to take the test. She went through the roof on prophecy.

Now think of the woman you know who speaks out

against injustice. "Who," asks Stuart Calvert, "warns against materialism and immorality? Who speaks out to say that Christian principles should apply to family life, sports, and politics?"

And who preaches the gospel with passion and power? That woman has the gift of prophecy.

2. SERVICE

Remember what Hendrix said service means: "serving people whatever they need—food, drink, clothing, shelter, jobs, care, love, and a million other things."

A gifted servant doesn't mind being behind the scenes, faithfully working in practical ways. But because the serving is behind the scenes, servants are not as documented as, say, a leader or a prophet. But we can still find some gifted ones in the Scriptures. Remember the widow of Zarephath who gave the last of her oil and meal to make a johnny cake for Elijah (1 Kings 17:9–16)?

In New Testament times, we hear of more examples. Paul often sent greetings to women who were laboring in the Lord. Dorcas, of course, was well known for her deed of kindness (Acts 9:36–41). Others who were cited as exceptional servants were Phoebe (Rom. 16:1), Tryphena (Rom. 16:12), and Persis (Rom. 16:12).

Modern-day servants make the world go around. One is Louise Barbour. At the first writing of this book, Louise was media designer at Woman's Missionary Union in Birmingham, Alabama. She has done a multitude of small, loving deeds for multitudes of people. She tackled pasteup jobs and layout work others dreaded. When other employees were out, she volunteered to help—even when she had work of her own to do. She would overhear an editor talking about a need for photographs and immediately make plans to take them. Her unbelievable visual aids and ideas for teaching mission studies were willingly shared.

Several years ago, her home church stole her away to direct their media program. But she continues to stretch her time and gifts to help those of us without an ounce of creativity.

Last summer, I taught sessions of *Yours for the Giving* at a large conference center. I needed to add a little pizzazz to the sessions, and was able to talk Louise into preparing 12 absolutely gorgeous posters—one for each of the service gifts. Although she was teaching three different sessions herself, she agreed to rescue this perishing friend.

I went to my conference room, however, minus posters. Where in the world was always dependable Louise? My cavernous room looked as inviting as a sepulchre. With a faltering voice (and heart), I began to teach. Ten words into my introduction, the door flew open and like a whirlwind, Louise charged into the room, casting posters helter-skelter. How un-Louise! But how like-Louise were the magnificent posters! "I had car trouble," she gasped.

"No problem," I exalted. "You just gave the world's best introduction to any conference I've ever done!"

Servants can be "gangbusters" sometimes.

Whom do you know who helps? She is a servant in your midst giving credibility to Christianity.

3. TEACHING

The gift of teaching, instructing, guiding, nurturing in the Word and will of God, is directed toward understanding. Who are those who help us understand?

During Bible days older women were expected to "teach what is good" (Titus 2:3). In 2 Timothy 1:5 Paul commends Timothy's grandmother, Lois, and his mother, Eunice, for their teaching. However, the best example of a female teacher-paragon during the New Testament times is Priscilla. She and her husband, Aquila, were friends of Paul. In Corinth they were fellow tentmakers. Paul stayed in their home. They became co-workers for the Lord.

A specific example of their teaching is found in Acts 18:24–26. An Egyptian Jew, Apollos, was in town preaching. He was an eloquent man and an Old Testament scholar. When Priscilla and Aquila heard Apollos they recognized that his teaching was incomplete. He knew about Jesus, but he didn't know of His death and resurrection. Priscilla and Aquila took Apollos aside and taught him about Jesus.

I have been blessed by some really great teachers. As a high school student, I had Ellen Ruth Smith. She taught biology and it was in that class that I recognized that God expected me to do my best.

But Ellen Ruth ("Teacher") was also my one of my teachers at church. It was those sessions with her that showed me my need for Christian growth. This remarkable teacher was my teacher, my mentor, and my friend.

Who in your circle of friends and acquaintances "turns on the light" and leads you to say, "I understand what you mean"? She is a gifted teacher.

4. EXHORTING

Exhorting is speaking out helpfully. It is the gift of counseling, the ability to give comforting and healing words to others, to encourage.

Two women encouraged Jesus not long before His crucifixion. Did they somehow sense that hard times were coming? Had they understood, as the disciples had not, of

His coming death? We read about the first woman in Luke 7:37–50. She anointed Jesus with oil. The second woman was Mary, the sister of Lazarus and Martha. Her loving gesture is recorded in John 12:18.

In fact, many women faithfully supported and ministered to Jesus. It has been fittingly said that women were last at the Cross and first at the tomb.

Paul sent greetings in most of his letters to women who supported his ministry, who labored with him, and who encouraged him. For instance, in Romans 16 Paul greeted 29 people in all. Ten are women.

One of the major agreements on spiritual gifts that Stuart Calvert and I share is on one of the great exhorters. The late Mary Essie Stephens served as executive director of Alabama Woman's Missionary Union when both of us were getting our feet wet in missions.

Mary Essie surely encouraged me. She recognized I had some abilities and gave me opportunities to teach and speak. It was also Mary Essie who led me to be involved in my first mission trip to Pittsburgh.

At the same time, she was encouraging Stuart, and many others, to be all that God wanted us to be.

To whom do you turn with an aching heart? Or who encourages you to say, "I can do that"? She is an exhorter.

5. SHARING

Who gives from an open heart, freely, with delight, with love? Immediately I think of the poor widow who gave all she had (Luke 21:1–4).

There were women who faithfully supplied Jesus and the disciples with money for their needs. Luke 8:3 names Joanna, the wife of Chuza, Herod's superintendent of royal properties, and Susanna.

I had the joy and honor of writing the biography of Gloria Thurman, a missionary to Bangladesh. While staying with the Thurmans in their home in Gopalgonj, I learned firsthand how sterling her gift of sharing is. Gloria believes that everything belongs to the Father. Their home is always open; their table is always crowded. Their garments can be spotted on men, women, and children. Even their empty bottles and cans are scattered in every home in the district. A cabbage from their garden feeds a family for days. Their money has purchased many wedding saris.

Simon Sicar, the president of the College of Christian Theology of Bangladesh speaks of Gloria's clinics. "Why does she do that? She thinks this is something she can do for the people and maybe she can get in their hearts and witness to them. If there is no medical need, she will give to others eggs, a tin of coffee, some fruit. It means she has thought about them. She loves them."

Gloria Thurman only knows how to share one way— with everything she has.

Who among your friends is always looking for ways to give? Who brings the casserole, even when it is not "her time to do it"? Who finds the time to take the shut-in to the grocery store? She is the gifted giver.

6. LEADING

A leader is able to organize, to motivate, to keep on keeping on.

Deborah was such a woman. So was Lydia. But perhaps the best example during Bible times was Phoebe. The first two verses of Romans 16 describe this extraordinary woman. Huber Drumwright gave an exciting description of Phoebe in his book *Saints Alive!* She was a friend of Paul and a member of the church at Cenchreae (a suburb of

Corinth). "This self-reliant woman, going to Rome on personal business it seems," Drumwright said, "was apparently entrusted with Paul's letter to the Romans." She was an inspiring Christian and a servant of the church at Cenchreae. *Servant* in Greek can be translated "deaconess." Paul further adds that Phoebe had been a supporter of many, including himself (Rom. 16:2).

In today's world, God has gifted some extraordinary women leaders. In the maelstrom of missionaries at a large conference center, men and women hawked their maps and curios and colorful lifestyles to throngs of curious onlookers. A petite brunette wearing a beautiful Malay costume drew people to her display. Her clear crisp explanations, her obvious love of her "adopted" country, her warm greetings to perfect strangers, made her a marked woman.

"She's a teacher," I recognized, "but she's more." Mentally I clicked through those earmarks of a leader: organized, confident when standing before others, hardworking, giving attention to details.

I saw this paragon, Linda Gaddis, solo in a jewel of a presentation in a Colorado meeting. She held us captive as she led us to see her Malaysia. In her explanations we glimpsed a trustworthy leader who led and welcomed fellow travelers and followers. What a leader!

Whom do you know who is willing to take responsibility? Who says, "I will try, if you will help"? She may be your leader.

7. MERCY

There are those who joyfully work with those the rest of us ignore: the deformed, crippled, mentally challenged, sick, aged, mentally ill. These have the gift of mercy.

Compassion is one of the most beautiful of the gifts for it is truly laced with love. Surely we can say of those women who waited at the Cross that they were merciful. Jesus was an outcast. Even His disciples, except John, fled.

But faithfully, agonizingly, the women kept watch. Matthew 27:55–56 (TEV) paints the scene at Golgotha: "There were many women there…who had followed Jesus from Galilee and helped him. Among them were Mary Magdalene, Mary the mother of James and Joseph, and the wife of Zebedee." They loved and ministered to the bitter end and then kept on loving. That is mercy.

I went to Bangladesh to write about a woman gifted in mercy, Gloria Thurman. While I was there I met Nirmala. During a women's retreat, Gloria and I taught *Yours for the Giving* at the insistence of the Bengali women. At the end of the teaching sessions every one of the 99 women attending identified her gifts.

The last to do so was a tiny, little old woman whose sari was wrapped around her so tightly not even the tip of her nose could be seen. She stood and pushed her sari away from her face.

I was not prepared to see a lovely young woman! But she was still very shy. She softly inquired of Gloria, "Ask the *memshaib* (me) if I have the gift of mercy?"

Gloria translated the question to me. "Ask her why she thinks she has the gift of mercy," I requested.

When Gloria relayed my message, Nirmala told this story: "I live in a little village. Two huts down from me, I have an elderly neighbor who has been very ill."

Nirmala described the illness and emphasized that the neighbor's right arm and hand (the eating hand in Bangladesh) trembled violently. When he attempted to bring his shaking fingers full of rice to his mouth, he'd lose it all before it reached its destination.

His daughter-in-law would say, "Look at you! Look at the mess you're making!" Then she would stick her hand into his bowl and jam a fistful of rice into his mouth. The rice would spill out the corners of his mouth and she'd say, "Look at you! Even when I go to all the trouble to feed you myself, you still make a mess!"

Then the young woman paused. Then she smiled and continued, "But—I have a spoon—a spoon of my own. So every day when my neighbor eats his one bowl of rice, I go with my spoon and I feed him, one spoon at a time. Before I know it, I'm scraping the bottom of the bowl and my neighbor smiles and says, 'Thank you. I am full.' And that makes me so happy. Is that the gift of mercy?"

Gloria and I both had tears streaming down our faces. "Oh, Gloria," I sobbed, "tell her that's the most beautiful gift of mercy I've ever heard about!"

Who in your circle of friends acts out good intentions? The merciful do not say, "If I can do anything, call me." They bandage the sores, they hug the stooped shoulders, and they rock the crying baby. They use their spoons.

8. Love

Here we are at love—the greatest of all Christian attributes. Whether or not we agree that love is a gift as well as part of the fruit of the Spirit, it is essential in the life of a Christian.

Jesus so outshines everyone in love. It is His character. But we can find examples in the Bible of others who exemplified love. Ruth loved in an extraordinary way. The Book of Ruth tells the story of her love and faithfulness to Naomi. Dorcas loved. All that crying when she died was not simply because they had lost a good seamstress. She was so important to the church in Joppa that Peter presented her back to them, alive (Acts 9:36–42)!

Some among us today have an extraordinary capacity to love. Thelma Bagby was one of those. Long before I reached this point in writing this book, I dreamed and plotted this chapter. To keep me going, I'd work on it a little while. One day I was thinking about the gift of love, and I thought, "That's Thelma Bagby!" The phone rang; Thelma Bagby said, "I don't have any reason for this call. I just want to tell you that I love you!" Talk about a sign from the Lord.

On January 3, 1996, Thelma went to be with the Father. But love as warm and wonderful as hers endures on and on and on.

Who, besides your mother, calls and says, "I love you"? Who shows that love in a million little ways to lots and lots of people? She has the gift of love.

9. ENTHUSIASM

The person with the gift of enthusiasm brings sparkle and excitement to whatever is happening. She gets excited!

I had a hard time finding an enthusiastic woman in the Bible. Martha got a little bit excited because Mary wouldn't help in the kitchen (Luke 10:40–42), but that wasn't what I had in mind! The other example is Rhoda. You remember her. When Peter knocked on the door, she went to answer it. She recognized Peter's voice, and got so excited that she forgot to open the door. She just ran to tell everyone that Peter was out of prison and at the door (Acts 12:12–16)!

I have two Texas friends who truly sparkle: Jeane Law from Lubbock and Debbie Ferrier from Houston. I would recognize their laughter across a crowded world (and especially in the Lone Star State)! Thank You, Lord, for enthusiastic friends like Jeane and Debbie.

Who do you know who "lights up the room"? Who

makes even the most ordinary event extra special? That woman has the gift of enthusiasm.

10. HOPE

One with hope is not easily disappointed in persons, and is able to bounce back from hard knocks.

A woman in the Bible who portrays hope to me is found in Luke 8:42–48. The story is about a woman who had been sick for 12 years. Hope must have dimmed during such a long illness. But it had not died. She made her way in the crowd wanting to simply touch the hem of the robe of Jesus. She knew that would be enough, and it was. "Daughter, your faith has healed you," Jesus told her (Luke 8:48).

Queen Esther had hope. She is known for her great courage, but she had hope, rooted in prayer and fasting (Esther 4:16).

The woman on my list who personifies hope is one who has endured. Her hope never dies. She is one of the most inspiring women I know.

Betty Rains served as a missionary with her husband, Randy, in Bangladesh. Guillain-Barré syndrome struck Randy. They returned home with Randy critically ill. After months of therapy, the paralysis was conquered. The Raines returned to Bangladesh. Again illness grabbed Randy. Again they returned to the United States. Undaunted, Betty and Randy went to Australia—a more moderate climate. One more time the Rains returned to Bangladesh. Once again illness struck. This time it was one of the children. The Rains family returned one more time to the US.

Betty's heart was broken. She accepted that they could not go back to Bangladesh. But her hope would not die. "Surely there is something I can do," she sobbed to me in a late night call. "And I think I know what it is. Someone must go to Bangladesh and follow Gloria Thurman around for a month and then come home and write her story."

So Betty's hope became her dream and it became a reality as I actually did go to Bangladesh and did try to introduce the world to Gloria, a true missionary, a true servant who incarnates the gospel.

Our prayer was that Gloria's story would inspire others as it had Betty. *Gloria!* was published in 1993. Since then Betty says she has personally encountered three new missionaries in training who say they sensed a call to missions after reading *Gloria!* Hope has multiplied!

Which one of your friends has been struck down, but rises again to face the world with God's help? Who never gives up? That woman personifies hope.

11. PRAYER

Some Christians have the special ability to pray for extended periods of time on a regular basis and see frequent and specific answers to their prayers.

Hannah was a prayer warrior. We can read of her prayer for a son in 1 Samuel 1 and 2. When Samuel was born, Hannah explained simply, "Because I asked the Lord for him" (1 Sam. 1:20).

Jesus told the story of another woman who knew how to ask in Luke 18:1–8. A poor widow kept coming to a corrupt judge saying: "Protect me!" (Luke 18:5 *The Message*). Finally, worn out, the judge granted the widow's request. Jesus concluded the story by saying, "So what makes you think God won't step in and work justice for His chosen people, who continue to cry out for help?" (Luke 18:7 *The Message*).

Edna Romero, a missionary in Taos, New Mexico, serves with her husband, Benny. Edna first heard about

Jesus from an Anglo missionary who came to her home pueblo, Santa Clara. The missionary was forbidden by the Indian governor to come back to Santa Clara. But Edna prayed for the Lord to send a missionary. Edna's mother, Rose Naranjo, heard her daughter's prayers day after day. "God answered Edna's prayers but in a way she never dreamed. God touched my heart," says Rose. "Then both Edna and I prayed for my husband, Mike, and he became a Christian. Not only did God save us, but He also called us to serve Him. When schooling was completed, God sent us back to Santa Clara, the first Indian missionaries to the Pueblo."

Which one of your friends prays with childlike trust, knowing God will answer? Who is faithful, asking again and again? She has the gift of prayer.

12. HOSPITALITY

Hospitality is that ability to provide open house and warm welcome for all who come your way.

William P. Barker gleaned from the Bible a lot of information about one of the most hospitable women during New Testament times—Mary, the mother of John Mark. "This Mary was a well-to-do woman in Jerusalem who became one of the earliest followers of Jesus. Her house became the unofficial meeting place for the earliest band of believers after the resurrection, and was probably the location of the 'Upper Room' in which the Last Supper was located. The disciples congregated there after the crucifixion and resurrection, prayed together at the time of Pentecost, and were worshipping there when James was put to death and Peter imprisoned."

Numerous house churches in New Testament times were held in the homes of hospitable women. The first church in Europe met in the home of Lydia (Acts 16:15, 40). The church in Rome met in the home of Priscilla and Aquila (Rom. 16:5), as had the church in Ephesus (Acts 18:2–6).

Today God's women continue to open their homes. Every missionary should be on this list because they are constant hostesses. They use their homes to establish relationships with persons in the community. Bible studies and even worship services are held in their living rooms.

I am luckier than most women. I travel with youth missions groups a great deal. I have a special love and appreciation for all the wonderful women who have taken us in on mission trips when we have been tired and dirty. They have fed us and tucked us in and made us feel loved.

In addition, I travel up and down the United States and even abroad speaking. I've stayed in thousands of homes. I've never felt anything but the very best kind of hospitality. Who do you know who takes home the stranger? Who always makes you feel welcome? Who opens her home to non-Christians and uses this as a way to lead them to Christ? She has the gift of hospitality.

Have you read this chapter and said again and again, "Who in the world is she? I don't know about that woman, but I wish Barbara Joiner knew my friend who *really does* have the gift of hospitality or service or prophecy." Good for you! That is exactly the reaction I want. Those women are gifted and are giving it away or you would never have noticed.

I have a missionary friend who served in the West African country of Nigeria. She sums up in a few sentences what I've taken a whole book to explain. Sandy Achenbach says, "The key to the gifts is the service they produce… in love. I've seen a lot of spiritually gifted people who use their gifts, but not in a service of love, and the services end up seeming so sad and forced." She adds, "It's too easy to keep our eyes on the gift and the service rather than on the gift giver and the spirit of service which is love."

So looking to the Father and reflecting His love, let us use our gifts to serve other persons and a lost world. The gifts are yours for the giving. They are like a beautiful flower that is native to Brazil. They never bloom until they are given away.

Questions to Think About

1. What have you learned about spiritual gifts that you did not know before you read this book?

2. What have you learned about yourself that you did not know before?

3. What is the difference between a talent and a spiritual gift?

4. What distinction do some people make between administration and leading?

5. Some people say that love should not be listed as a spiritual gift. Why? Do you agree or disagree?

6. What gifted person described in this book impressed you most?

7. Write a paragraph each about three persons you know who are using their spiritual gifts.

8. What role in ministry will you take because of reading this book?

9. What change will you make in your daily activities because of reading this book?

NOTES